A Most Jubilant Song

Walt Whitman

A Most Jubilant Song

Inspiring Writings About the Wonderful World Around Us

Selected by Shifra Stein

♛ Hallmark Crown Editions

Titles set in Goudy Cursive and text set in Goudy Old Style.
Printed on Hallmark Buff Vellux Book paper.
Designed by Ronald E. Garman.
Copyright © 1973 by Hallmark Cards, Inc.,
Kansas City, Missouri. All Rights Reserved.
Printed in the United States of America.
Library of Congress Catalog Card Number: 72-83614.
Standard Book Number: 87529-316-6.

Walt Whitman (1819-1892)

While on an extensive tour of the United States in 1847-48, Walt Whitman conceived the idea of writing a book of verses that would interpret the "American dream" as he had come to understand it. "The United States themselves," he decided, "are essentially the greatest poem."

In 1855 the poet brought out the first edition of Leaves of Grass — a much-praised 94-page volume that he spent the rest of his life revising and enlarging. All of the poems that follow are taken from the sixth — and final — edition, published in 1892, and the prose selections from his several other books.

Whitman found form for his thoughts in the objects of nature. And while the poems advocate a doctrine of individualism, they also promote the ideas of companionship and brotherhood.

In Whitman's later years, he devoted himself to humanitarian causes. He died in 1892, having bequeathed to the American people a book full of good cheer, hope and comradeship.

"O to make the most jubilant song!/Full of music — full of manhood, womanhood, infancy!" he wrote. And that is the spirit of this new volume, captured in the words of the author and with memorable photographs of the America of Whitman's day.

Earth Lover

Smile O voluptuous cool-breath'd earth!
Earth of the slumbering and liquid trees!
Earth of departed sunset — earth of the mountains misty-topt!
Earth of the vitreous pour of the full moon just tinged with blue!
Earth of shine and dark mottling the tide of the river!
Earth of the limpid gray of clouds brighter and clearer for my sake!
Far-swooping elbow'd earth — rich apple-blossom'd earth!
Smile, for your lover comes.

Unseen Buds

Unseen buds, infinite, hidden well,
Under the snow and ice, under the darkness, in every square or cubic inch,
Germinal, exquisite, in delicate lace, microscopic, unborn,
Like babes in wombs, latent, folded, compact, sleeping;
Billions of billions, and trillions of trillions of them waiting,
(On earth and in the sea — the universe — the stars there in the heavens,)
Urging slowly, surely forward, forming endless,
And waiting ever more, forever more behind.

The Road Is Before Us

Allons! the road is before us!

It is safe — I have tried it — my own feet have tried it well — be not detain'd!
Let the paper remain on the desk unwritten, and the book on the shelf unopen'd!

Let the tools remain in the workshop! let the money remain unearn'd!
Let the school stand! mind not the cry of the teacher!
Let the preacher preach in his pulpit! let the lawyer plead in the court,
    and the judge expound the law.

Camerado, I give you my hand!
I give you my love more precious than money,
I give you myself before preaching or law;
Will you give me yourself? will you come travel with me?
Shall we stick by each other as long as we live?

The Common Earth, the Soil

The soil, too — let others pen-and-ink the sea, the air, (as I sometimes try) —
but now I feel to choose the common soil for theme — naught else.
The brown soil here, (just between winter-close and opening spring and vegetation) —
the rain-shower at night, and the fresh smell next morning —
the red worms wriggling out of the ground — the dead leaves, the incipient grass,
and the latent life underneath — the effort to start something — already in shelter'd spots
some little flowers — the distant emerald show of winter wheat and the rye fields —
the yet naked trees, with clear interstices, giving prospects hidden in summer —
the tough fallow and the plow-team, and the stout boy whistling to his horses
for encouragement — and there the dark fat earth in long slanting stripes upturn'd.

For You O Democracy

Come, I will make the continent indissoluble,
I will make the most splendid race the sun ever shone upon,
I will make divine magnetic lands,
    With the love of comrades,
        With the life-long love of comrades.

I will plant companionship thick as trees along all
    the rivers of America, and along the shores of the great
    lakes, and all over the prairies,
I will make inseparable cities with their arms about each other's necks,
    By the love of comrades,
        By the manly love of comrades,

For you these from me, O Democracy, to serve you ma femme!
For you, for you I am trilling these songs.

On the Beach at Night

On the beach at night,
Stands a child with her father,
Watching the east, the autumn sky.

Up through the darkness,
While ravening clouds, the burial clouds, in black masses spreading,
Lower sullen and fast athwart and down the sky,
Amid a transparent clear belt of ether yet left in the east,
Ascends large and calm the lord-star Jupiter,
And nigh at hand, only a very little above,
Swim the delicate sisters the Pleiades.

From the beach the child holding the hand of her father,
Those burial clouds that lower victorious soon to devour all,
Watching, silently weeps.

Weep not, child,
Weep not, my darling,
With these kisses let me remove your tears,
The ravening clouds shall not long be victorious,
They shall not long possess the sky, they devour the stars only in apparition,
Jupiter shall emerge, be patient, watch again another night, the Pleiades shall emerge,
They are immortal, all those stars both silvery and golden shall shine out again,
The great stars and the little ones shall shine out again, they endure,
The vast immortal suns and the long-enduring pensive moons shall again shine....

Women in America

Democracy, in silence, biding its time, ponders its own ideals, not of literature and art only —
not of men only, but of women. The idea of the women of America, (extricated from this daze,
this fossil and unhealthy air which hangs about the word *lady)* developed, raised to become
the robust equals, workers, and, it may be, even practical and political deciders with the men —
greater than man, we may admit, through their divine maternity, always their towering,
emblematic attribute — but great, at any rate, as man, in all departments; or, rather,
capable of being so, soon as they realize it, and can bring themselves to give up toys and fictions,
and launch forth, as men do, amid real, independent, stormy life.

Beautiful Women

Women sit or move to and fro, some old, some young,
The young are beautiful — but the old are more beautiful than the young.

Poetry in Cities

The splendor, picturesqueness, and oceanic amplitude and rush of these great cities,
the unsurpassed situation, rivers and bay, sparkling sea-tides, costly and lofty new buildings,
facades of marble and iron, of original grandeur and elegance of design, with the masses of gay color,
the preponderance of white and blue, the flags flying, the endless ships,
the tumultuous streets…these, I say, and the like of these, completely satisfy my senses of power,
fullness, motion, and give me, through such senses and appetites,
and through my aesthetic conscience, a continued exaltation and absolute fulfillment.

Two Rivulets

Two Rivulets side by side,
Two blended, parallel, strolling tides,
Companions, travelers, gossiping as they journey.

For the Eternal Ocean bound,
These ripples, passing surges, streams of Death and Life.

Object and Subject hurrying, whirling by,
The Real and Ideal,

Alternate ebb and flow the Days and Nights,
(Strands of a Trio twining, Present, Future, Past.)

In You, whoever you are, my book perusing,
In I myself — in all the World — these ripples flow,
All, all, toward the mystic Ocean tending.

(O yearnful waves! the kisses of your lips!
Your breast so broad, with open arms, O firm, expanded shore!)

Faces

Sauntering the pavement or riding the country by-road, lo, such faces!
Faces of friendship, precision, caution, suavity, ideality,
The spiritual-prescient face, the always welcome common benevolent face,
The face of the singing of music, the grand faces of natural lawyers
      and judges broad at the back-top,
The faces of hunters and fishers bulged at the brows, the shaved blanch'd faces of orthodox citizens,
The pure, extravagant, yearning, questioning artist's face,
The ugly face of some beautiful soul, the handsome detested or despised face,
The sacred faces of infants, the illuminated face of the mother of many children,
The face of an amour, the face of veneration,
The face as of a dream, the face of an immobile rock,
The face withdrawn of its good and bad, a castrated face,
A wild hawk, his wings clipp'd by the clipper,
A stallion that yielded at last to the thongs and knife of the gelder.

Sauntering the pavement thus, or crossing the ceaseless ferry, faces and faces and faces,
I see them and complain not, and am content with all.

A Farm Picture

Through the ample open door of the peaceful country barn,
A sunlit pasture field with cattle and horses feeding,
And haze and vista, and the far horizon fading away.

The Work of Man

I realize that not Nature alone is great in her fields of freedom and the open air, in her storms,
the shows of night and day, the mountains, forests, sea — but in the artificial,
the work of man too is equally great — in this profusion of teeming humanity — in these ingenuities,
streets, goods, houses, ships — these hurrying, feverish, electric crowds of men, their complicated
business genius…and all this mighty, many-threaded wealth and industry concentrated here.

Echoes

The house-builder at work in cities or anywhere,
The preparatory jointing, squaring, sawing, mortising,
The hoist-up of beams, the push of them in their places, laying them regular,
Setting the studs by their tenons in the mortises according as they were prepared,
The blows of mallets and hammers, the attitudes of the men, their curv'd limbs,
Bending, standing, astride the beams, driving in pins, holding on by posts and braces,
The hook'd arm over the plate, the other arm wielding the axe,
The floor-men forcing the planks close to be nail'd,
Their postures bringing their weapons downward on the bearers,
The echoes resounding through the vacant building....

The main shapes arise!
Shapes of Democracy total, result of centuries,
Shapes ever projecting other shapes,
Shapes of turbulent manly cities,
Shapes of the friends and home-givers of the whole earth,
Shapes bracing the earth and braced with the whole earth.

A Song of Joys

O to make the most jubilant song!
Full of music — full of manhood, womanhood, infancy!
Full of common employments — full of grain and trees.

O for the voices of animals — O for the swiftness and balance of fishes!
O for the dropping of raindrops in a song!
O for the sunshine and motion of waves in a song!

O the joy of my spirit — it is uncaged — it darts like lightning!
It is not enough to have this globe or a certain time,
I will have thousands of globes and all time.

O the engineer's joys! to go with a locomotive!
To hear the hiss of steam, the merry shriek, the steam whistle, the laughing locomotive!
To push with resistless way and speed off in the distance.

O the gleesome saunter over fields and hillsides!
The leaves and flowers of the commonest weeds, the moist fresh stillness of the woods,
The exquisite smell of the earth at daybreak, and all through the forenoon.

O the horseman's and horsewoman's joys!
The saddle, the gallop, the pressure upon the seat, the cool gurgling by the ears and hair.

O the fireman's joys!
I hear the alarm at dead of night,
I hear bells, shouts! I pass the crowd, I run!
The sight of the flames maddens me with pleasure.

O the mother's joys!
The watching, the endurance, the precious love, the anguish, the patiently yielded life.

O the joy of increase, growth, recuperation,
The joy of soothing and pacifying, the joy of concord and harmony.

O to go back to the place where I was born,
To hear the birds sing once more,
To ramble about the house and barn and over the fields once more,
And through the orchard and along the old lanes once more.

O the old manhood of me, my noblest joy of all!
My children and grand-children, my white hair and beard,
My largeness, calmness, majesty, out of the long stretch of my life.

O ripen'd joy of womanhood! O happiness at last!
I am more than eighty years of age, I am the most venerable mother,
How clear is my mind—how all people draw nigh to me!
What attractions are these beyond any before? what bloom more than the bloom of youth?
What beauty is this that descends upon me and rises out of me?

O the orator's joys!
To inflate the chest, to roll the thunder of the voice out from the ribs and throat,
To make the people rage, weep, hate, desire, with yourself,
To lead America — to quell America with a great tongue.

O the farmer's joys!
Ohioan's, Illinoisian's, Wisconsinese', Kanadian's, Iowan's, Kansian's, Missourian's, Oregonese' joys!
To rise at peep of day and pass forth nimbly to work,
To plough land in the fall for winter-sown crops,
To plough land in the spring for maize,
To train orchards, to graft the trees, to gather apples in the fall.

O to bathe in the swimming-bath, or in a good place along shore,
To splash the water! to walk ankle-deep, or race naked along the shore.

O to realize space!
The plenteousness of all, that there are no bounds,
To emerge and be of the sky, of the sun and moon and flying clouds, as one with them.

O to have life henceforth a poem of new joys!
To dance, clap hands, exult, shout, skip, leap, roll on, float on!
To be a sailor of the world bound for all ports,
A ship itself, (see indeed these sails I spread to the sun and air,)
A swift and swelling ship full of rich words, full of joys.

The Sky--Days and Nights--Happiness

A clear, crispy day — dry and breezy air, full of oxygen. Out of the sane, silent,
beauteous miracles that envelope and fuse me — trees, water, grass, sunlight, and early frost —
the one I am looking at most to-day is the sky. It has that delicate, transparent blue,
peculiar to autumn, and the only clouds are little or larger white ones, giving their still and
spiritual motion to the great concave. All through the earlier day (say from 7 to 11) it keeps a pure,
yet vivid blue. But as noon approaches the color gets lighter, quite gray for two or three hours —
then still paler for a spell, till sundown — which last I watch dazzling through the interstices
of a knoll of big trees — darts of fire and a gorgeous show of light-yellow, liver-color and red,
with a vast silver glaze askant on the water — the transparent shadows, shafts, sparkle,
and vivid colors beyond all the paintings ever made.

Two Together

Shine! shine! shine!
Pour down your warmth, great sun!
While we bask, we two together,

Two together!
Winds blow south, or winds blow north,
Day come white, or night come black,
Home, or rivers and mountains from home,
Singing all time, minding no time,
While we two keep together.

Youth

Youth, large, lusty, loving—youth full of grace, force, fascination,
Do you know that Old Age may come after you with equal grace, force, fascination?

39

What Is the Grass?

A child said *What is the grass?* fetching it to me with full hands,
How could I answer the child? I do not know what it is any more than he.

I guess it must be the flag of my disposition, out of hopeful green stuff woven.

Or I guess it is the handkerchief of the Lord,
A scented gift and remembrancer designedly dropt,
Bearing the owner's name someway in the corners, that we may see and remark, and say *Whose?*

Or I guess the grass is itself a child, the produced babe of the vegetation.

To a Locomotive in Winter

Thee for my recitative,
Thee in the driving storm even as now, the snow, the winter-day declining,
Thee in thy panoply, thy measur'd dual throbbing and thy beat convulsive,
Thy black cylindric body, golden brass and silvery steel,
Thy ponderous side-bars, parallel and connecting rods, gyrating, shuttling at thy sides,
Thy metrical, now swelling pant and roar, now tapering in the distance,
Thy great protruding head-light fix'd in front,
Thy long, pale, floating vapor-pennants, tinged with delicate purple,
The dense and murky clouds out-belching from thy smoke-stack,
Thy knitted frame, thy springs and valves, the tremulous twinkle of thy wheels,
Thy train of cars behind, obedient, merrily following,
Through gale or calm, now swift, now slack, yet steadily careering;
Type of the modern — emblem of motion and power — pulse of the continent,
For once come serve the Muse and merge in verse, even as here I see thee,
With storm and buffeting gusts of wind and falling snow,
By day thy warning ringing bell to sound its notes,
By night thy silent signal lamps to swing.

Fierce-throated beauty!
Roll through my chant with all thy lawless music, thy swinging lamps at night,
Thy madly-whistled laughter, echoing, rumbling like an earthquake, rousing all,
Law of thyself complete, thine own track firmly holding,
(No sweetness debonair of tearful harp or glib piano thine,)
Thy trills of shrieks by rocks and hills return'd,
Launch'd o'er the prairies wide, across the lakes,
To the free skies unpent and glad and strong.

Night on the Prairies

Night on the prairies,
The supper is over, the fire on the ground burns low,
The wearied emigrants sleep, wrapt in their blankets;
I walk by myself — I stand and look at the stars, which I think now I never realized before.

Now I absorb immortality and peace,
I admire death and test propositions.

How plenteous! how spiritual! how resumé!
The same old man and soul — the same old aspirations, and the same content.

I was thinking the day most splendid till I saw what the not-day exhibited,
I was thinking this globe enough till there sprang out so noiseless around me myriads of other globes.

Now while the great thoughts of space and eternity fill me I will measure myself by them,
And now touch'd with the lives of other globes arrived as far along as those of the earth,
Or waiting to arrive, or pass'd on farther than those of the earth,
I henceforth no more ignore them than I ignore my own life,
Or the lives of the earth arrived as far as mine, or waiting to arrive.

O I see now that life cannot exhibit all to me, as the day cannot,
I see that I am to wait for what will be exhibited by death.

One's-Self I Sing

One's-Self I sing, a simple separate person,
Yet utter the word Democratic, the word En-Masse.

Of physiology from top to toe I sing,
Not physiognomy alone nor brain alone is worthy for the Muse,
    I say the Form complete is worthier far,
The Female equally with the Male I sing.

Of Life immense in passion, pulse, and power,
Cheerful, for freest action form'd under the laws divine,
The Modern Man I sing.

A Race of Singers

I say no land or people or circumstances ever existed so needing a race of singers and poems
differing from all others, and rigidly their own, as the land and people and circumstances
of our United States need such singers and poems today, and for the future.

Animals

I think I could turn and live with animals, they're so placid and self-contain'd,
I stand and look at them long and long.

They do not sweat and whine about their condition,
They do not lie awake in the dark and weep for their sins,
They do not make me sick discussing their duty to God,
Not one is dissatisfied, not one is demented with the mania of owning things,
Not one kneels to another, nor to his kind that lived thousands of years ago,
Not one is respectable or unhappy over the whole earth.

I Saw in Louisiana a Live-Oak Growing

I saw in Louisiana a live-oak growing,
All alone stood it and the moss hung down from the branches,
Without any companion it grew there uttering joyous leaves of dark green,
And its look, rude, unbending, lusty, made me think of myself,
But I wonder'd how it could utter joyous leaves
      standing alone there without its friend near, for I knew I could not,
And I broke off a twig with a certain number of leaves upon it, and twined around it a little moss,
And brought it away, and I have placed it in sight in my room,
It is not needed to remind me as of my own dear friends,
(For I believe lately I think of little else than of them,)
Yet it remains to me a curious token, it makes me think of manly love;
For all that, and though the live-oak glistens there in Louisiana solitary in a wide flat space,
Uttering joyous leaves all its life without a friend a lover near,
I know very well I could not.

Thanks in Old Age

Thanks in old age — thanks ere I go,
For health, the midday sun, the impalpable air — for life, mere life,
For precious ever-lingering memories, (of you my mother dear — you father —
    you, brothers, sisters, friends,)
For all my days — not those of peace alone — the days of war the same,
For gentle words, caresses, gifts from foreign lands,
For shelter, wine and meat — for sweet appreciation,
(You distant, dim unknown — or young or old — countless, unspecified, readers belov'd,
We never met, and ne'er shall meet — and yet our souls embrace, long, close and long;)
For beings, groups, love, deeds, words, books — for colors, forms,
For all the brave strong men — devoted, hardy men — who've forward sprung
    in freedom's help, all years, all lands,
For braver, stronger, more devoted men — (a special laurel ere I go, to life's war's chosen ones,
The cannoneers of song and thought — the great artillerists —
    the foremost leaders, captains of the soul:)
As soldier from an ended war return'd — As traveler out of myriads,
    to the long procession retrospective,
Thanks — joyful thanks! — a soldier's, traveler's thanks.

A Noiseless Patient Spider

A noiseless patient spider,
I mark'd where on a little promontory it stood isolated,
Mark'd how to explore the vacant vast surrounding,
It launch'd forth filament, filament, filament, out of itself,
Ever unreeling them, ever tirelessly speeding them.

And you O my soul where you stand,
Surrounded, detached, in measureless oceans of space,
Ceaselessly musing, venturing, throwing, seeking the spheres to connect them,
Till the bridge you will need be form'd, till the ductile anchor hold,
Till the gossamer thread you fling catch somewhere, O my soul.

I Dream'd in a Dream

I dream'd in a dream I saw a city invincible to the attacks of the whole of the rest of the earth,
I dream'd that was the new city of Friends,
Nothing was greater there than the quality of robust love, it led the rest,
It was seen every hour in the actions of the men of that city,
And in all their looks and words.

A Great City

A great city is that which has the greatest men and women,
If it be a few ragged huts it is still the greatest city in the whole world.

59

One Song, America, Before I Go

One song, America, before I go,
I'd sing, o'er all the rest, with trumpet sound,
For thee — the Future.

I'd sow a seed for thee of endless Nationality;
I'd fashion thy Ensemble, including Body and Soul;
I'd show, away ahead, the real Union, and how it may be accomplish'd.
(The paths to the House I seek to make,
But leave to those to come, the House itself.)

Belief I sing — and Preparation;
As Life and Nature are not great with reference to the Present only,
But greater still from what is to come,
Out of that formula for Thee I sing.